RILEY AN1

EXCERPTS FROM THE DIARY

OF A

BRIDLINGTON CAT

By

Anthony Healey

Riley was a rescued cat. Dumped into the North Sea inside a rubbish sack, saved by inquisitive gulls who brought the sack ashore, then taken home by a kind couple who gave him safe refuge. Unfortunately, they had a dog which didn't take kindly to sharing his space with a cat. Especially an intelligent one. Their first few months together and Riley's subsequent departure are narrated in Riley's diary...

RILEY ANTHONY

This book is a work of fiction

Names, characters places and incidents are a product of the author's imagination or are used fictitiously.

Any resemblance to actual peoples living or dead apart from Shezza and Riley are purely coincidental.

Anthony Healey November 2013

For Cheryl

With a little help from Riley, and a lot of help from Helen.

CONTENTS.   Page

PROLOGUE

I just knew that 2014 would be a completely different year to those gone by. I could feel it in my whiskers. How right I was. As the days, weeks and months began to unfurl, so did life as I knew it.

HI! I'm Riley Anthony. I'm a cat. Not just any old moggie. *I,* am a Bridlington Tabby cat and proud of it. Though I say it myself, we are a tough breed out here, fronting onto the North Sea in the winter months with its mountainous waves, biting cold winds and freezing mist or 'fret' as we refer to it. It can soon have you 'fretting', when it sweeps in from the sea, enveloping all before it. You can throw anything you like at a Bridlington cat and we will tough it out under the harshest of conditions; although it would help if someone threw a lump of cod or haddock now and then. But the winters months are short lived and soon change into glorious long summer days when a cat can enjoy the wonderful atmosphere of this great resort.

Bridlington is nestled in a bay on the edge of the North Sea in the East Riding of Yorkshire, often overlooked by travellers heading for the busier Towns of Scarborough and Whitby. And that's just the way we cats like it. To stroll down to the fantastic beaches and decide whether to snooze or surf without having your tail trodden on is *so* relaxing. So let's keep this between ourselves and don't go spreading the word about this Holiday Haven. More crowds mean more feet, and more tails squashed.

Bridlington has a small harbour where Fishing boats tie up and unload their 'catch'. There are always a few tasty fishbits to be had around the gutting sheds, but first you have to get past 'Jellybone Frazer' and his gang of flea-bitten mates. They jealously guard the road entrance to the gutting sheds and are some of the roughest cats I have ever come across. Even if you get past Jelly's gang (the undead), you still have to run the gauntlet with the Seagulls who follow the boats in and make first claim. I personally have lost a clump or two of my hide to those scavengers, but it's worth it to get close to the gutting shed waste bins where you can eat yourself silly. Then when you have filled your belly, you have to get back past 'Jelly', and that's no mean feat when your stomach is dragging along the harbour wall. But Hey! What would life be without a little skin and fur flying in all directions?

ONE

JANUARY 2014. Happy new year???...

When 2013 ended I thought, oh, well, another year gone and the same again to look forward to. How wrong I was. This has been the strangest year ever for me. A rollercoaster of excitement, fear, love and hate. Most important of all, the year that I was introduced to 'Shezza', the tea shop lady with a welcoming smile and a heart of gold. Then, as if that wasn't enough I went on to meet Lydia! OH, Lydia! Lydia! Lydia! Gosh, I still can't say her name without a tremor in my voice. To say Hello and goodbye to such a wonderful creature in just a couple of days has really knocked the frizz out of *my* fur.

Looking back, things started changing soon after Rufus kidnapped the Christmas Turkey. . .

TWO.

DECEMBER 25th 2013. *Dinner is…er, not served…*

Rufus is a big stupid mutt of a dog who I share house with along with Mr. and Mrs. who feed us. In return for being fed and watered I try to keep them entertained by showing them a few tricks. Juggling a ball, chasing spiders, snuggling up to them when they are cold and lifting their spirits if they seem down. My best trick is opening doors for them by leaping up and grabbing the handle. A quick twist with my paws and Hey Presto! Doors open.

Rufus on the other hand entertains them by chewing the furniture, chair legs, edges of carpet and anything else that takes his fancy. His latest trick entitled 'The disappearing Turkey' was the last straw. Even worse was the fact that I ended up taking the blame for him.

I know it's traditional that everybody gets a Turkey ten times bigger than they need and have to conjure up a thousand ways to make it into exciting meals for the next fortnight. Mr. and Mrs. Were saved from all of that, courtesy of Rufus and his amazing elastic stomach, although it seems, it was all, my fault.

THREE.

December 25th 2013. *Cat in the doghouse.*

The kitchen is the busiest room on Christmas day. To help out I make myself scarce until all the food is prepared. Curled up on the window ledge in the front room, soaking up the remains of the winter sun through the glass and studying the inside of my eyelids is my favourite pastime.

Rufus was worrying a defenseless slipper behind the sofa. Mr. and Mrs. were in the kitchen, setting the table for dinner. The sound of the oven door opening and closing was music to my ears. Mrs. always cooked the giblets from the turkey and that was a treat for Rufus and me.

At last it was time for the steaming turkey to be removed from the oven and placed onto the worktop to cool. That was the moment when things began to go pear shaped.

The doorbell started chiming. Rufus howled and barked as loud as he could to warn Mr. and Mrs. of an impending invasion. 'No turkey for you if you don't be quiet,' Mrs. jabbed a finger at him. That struck him dumb apart from the usual sad whimpering he does

17

when he knows he's done something wrong. Glancing out, I recognized the figures on the path.

Oh no, I thought, it's that fellow Quentin and his weird wife Hermione from next door inviting Mr. and Mrs. round for Christmas Aperitifs. Aperitifs? This is Brid. Sonny Jim, not the bloomin Bahamas!

Quentin and Hermione emigrated from Barnsley on a cheap away day offer by rail last year and decided to stay rather than waste money on the fare home. That's their story anyway. They seem to think that they are the trendsetters of the area.

'Ooh, we were just getting our dinner ready', said Mrs. 'What do you think Mr.?'

'Well, I suppose it will give the turkey time to cool and make it easier to carve' replied Mr.

'Okay then,' said Mrs., 'shut the kitchen door while these two are in the front room'. With a 'we won't be long', they went out. 'What about our giblets'? me and Rufus moaned.

Hours later, well at least twenty minutes, we were aware of the delicious aroma of cooked turkey, crackling and most important, roast giblets creeping under the kitchen door and invading our noses. It became more than cat and dog could stand. Trying to ignore it, I stared out of the window for a while hoping to see Mr. and Mrs. returning. Rufus joined me and we watched closely as

'Trudge Trenchmouth' who lives across the road from us let his scabby hound 'Snotter' out of his front door to run across and do his 'business' in our garden. But we weren't watching 'Snotter'. We were staring at Trudge, or rather, what he held in his hand. It was a huge turkey leg, dripping grease down to his elbow, as he slurped away at it with his toothless gums. After sucking at it like an ice lolly for a while, Trudge threw it to the apple of his eye, Snotter, who lived up to his name and drenched the street in saliva. He's one of those dribbling bulldog types who look like they've been hit head on by a bus and almost had their head forced out of their backside. Dribbling was what he did with dedication. He could put out a bush fire just by shaking his head vigorously, and now he had a turkey leg to chew on he got down to some serious dribbling. When he went back inside you could be excused for thinking that a giant snail had passed through the area….

After the entertainment, my mind went straight back to turkey and giblets. I was growing rather peckish and there was still no sign of Mr. and Mrs. I supposed that Quentin was probably boring them rigid with his daring and death defying adventures while big game hunting in upper Barnsley. I pondered over what to do for ages and ages, well at least twenty seconds. Seeing as the giblets were for us, and Mr. and Mrs. had gone out in a rush, forgetting to give them to us, why not save them the trouble and get them myself?

Convincing myself that Mrs. would come back in and say 'what a clever cat, Mr., he's gone and fed themselves because we were gone ages, drinking with our wonderful neighbours', I performed my party trick, leaping up the kitchen door, grasping the handle. After a little twisting the door swung open taking me with it and leaving a wide gap. That gap was suddenly filled with a Rufus I have never observed before. Moving faster than the speed of light, as if 'Snotter' had chomped on his tail, he burst into the kitchen and headed straight for the turkey. Before I could say 'the giblets are over here,' both turkey and plate were crashing down from the worktop and onto the floor. He then proceeded to drag it into the front room and behind the sofa, where he set about it with gusto. When I attempted to get it away from him, the tripehound clobbered me with his dinner plate sized feet. I gave up and went back to the kitchen for my giblets. Rufus stayed behind the sofa with his prize, chomping away like starving Marvin. After eating my share of the giblets I curled up near to the warm oven and though I tried hard not to, I fell asleep.

I awoke to the sound of the front door opening and the voices of Quentin and Hermione saying 'We didn't realize it was still frozen. We put it out to thaw ages ago. It's very good of you to invite us to share yours.'

'That's what neighbours are for' replied Mrs.   'Have you got lots of roast potatoes?' Trilled Hermione. 'And plum pudding to follow?' This from an excited Quentin.

I waited with bated breath. It was quite dark by now and someone turned on the light. 'OH MY GOOD GAWD!' Screamed Mrs. 'HAVE WE HAD BURGLARS?' 'Blooming cat burglars more like,' growled Mr. pointing at the kitchen door, and me emerging sleepily toward them.   Upon entering the front room I could hardly believe my eyes. While I was snoozing Rufus must have wrestled the turkey all over the place, leaving a trail of skin and bones across the furniture and carpets, ending in a grand finale of leftovers and the Carcase all piled up into---*no—no—NO! NOT MY BASKET!* 'Yes I'm afraid so' said the sly look in Rufus's eyes as I caught sight of him behind the sofa feigning sleep, his stomach the size of a potbellied pig.

'That cat has got to go!' Yelled Mr. 'He's far too clever for his own good.'   .
'It might not be all Rileys doing,' said Mrs. 'the two of them were in here'.
'Yes, but who can open doors?' Replied Mr. 'and anyway, Rufus is still asleep behind the sofa. He probably hasn't budged since we went out'. I turned to appeal to the treacherous tripehound and he rewarded me with a quick leer before snoring loudly. 'There look, he hasn't woken up yet' concluded Mr.

'Does this mean there's no turkey dinner?' wailed Quentin, 'I was really looking forward to it.'

'Not unless you want to wash the scraps under the tap' growled Mr.

'Perhaps we could have a sprout and roast potato sandwich?' offered Hermione.

'Or perhaps we could go back next door and work on de-frosting that bird of yours' said Mr.

'Oh maybe not,' blustered Quentin, heading toward the door, 'I can feel one of my migraines coming on, I need a head massage. Come along Hermione, I need your delicate touch.' And with that they were out of the door and gone.

'Perhaps it's not all bad news then,' said Mrs. starting to clean up the mess, 'at least it got rid of those two.'

Mr. nodded in agreement 'there's someone else we might need to be rid of too, if he pulls one more trick like this.' All eyes were on me.

I appeared to be in the doghouse for a couple of hours with both Mr. and Mrs. ignoring me. They were watching television after Mrs. had salvaged what she could of the turkey and cobbled together a makeshift meal. Rufus was still behind the sofa and really asleep by now. He suddenly awoke, howling, followed by deep moaning, followed closely by projectile vomiting......

And so began the unwanted redecoration of the front room in a sickly beigey turkeyish colour.

FOUR.

February 2014. *Manchester Shezza .*

Mrs. worked part time at a café in the town centre, close to where the popular weekly markets are held. A few weeks after our Christmas antics, she came home one afternoon and announced to Mr. 'Shezza, at work was telling me that she used to keep cats before she came to Brid. And she really misses the company. I was wondering if Riley would take to her.' *WHATS THAT? I gasped. Who might this Shezza be? Where does she live? Is her place clean and comfy enough for me? Will she get my favourite food and treats? Although, I haven't had many treats lately.* The poorly Rufus has been getting all those because his delicate stomach won't accept normal food. 'Might be worth a try,' growled Mr. 'After the expense it cost to put the front room right. To say nothing of the vets fees for Rufus's stomach repairs. That cat has cost us a pretty penny.'

I can't believe that I am still carrying the can for that greedy Tripehound. Mrs. said 'I'll have a word with her tomorrow at work; she's a nice hardworking girl, from Manchester, apparently.' *Manchester? Where is that? Definitely not in Yorkshire. Are Manchesterans or whatever they are called, civilized? Perhaps she'll fatten me up and use me instead of a Christmas turkey!*

AGHH! I've got turkey on the brain. I need a lie down in a darkened room.

A few days later Mrs. informed Mr. that Manchester Shezza would call round one day after work to be introduced, as she delicately put it, 'to our little furry problem.' Problem? I've been called some things in my time but never a problem. I'm not a problem cat. I just live with a scheming problem mutt who offloads all his misdeeds onto me. I decided there and then that I wouldn't leave my cozy home because of that four legged dimwit, and furthermore I would not take kindly to this Shezza person. I would scratch her legs, bite her hands and do anything I could to put her off me. My sole intentions now were to ingratiate myself back into the good books of Mr. and Mrs. I was going nowhere.

One week later. Friday evening 6.15.

It was cold, crispy and dark outside. Snug and warm by the fire, inside. I was watching television engrossed in local Bridlington news and the price of fish in the European Community when the doorbell sounded. Mrs. was busy in the kitchen preparing the evening meal. Mr. struggled reluctantly from his armchair to see who it was. I darted quickly into his vacant seat to see if I could keep it warm for him. 'Probably bloomin canvassers' he grumbled as he opened the door with his usual punch line, 'we don't want none,' which is a contradiction anyway, 'whatever it is that you're selling.'

'I'm not selling anything' was the reply with a gentle laugh, in a soft, warm husky voice that made my tail tingle. Curiosity being my middle name, I just had to go and take a peek. WOW! What a bobby dazzler. I would buy anything from this canvasser just to keep her at the door while I breathed her presence in. Long blonde hair, big blue eyes, a smile that just oozed friendliness and the body of an angel, made for cuddling. Mr. was mesmerized, with a stupid grin on his face, while I was thinking that Manchester Shezza, if she ever showed up would be a great obnoxious frump compared with this vision of beauty. 'And I'm not voting for Clifton Bladderhead if that's who you are canvassing for.' Mr. had finally found his voice albeit a bit squeaky. 'He did nowt for us pensioners last time! I might as well have voted for Wesley Windbag, of the save our sausage party for all the good it did.'

The Angel spoke again 'I don't think its election time and I've actually come to meet Riley Anthony, if that's okay with you?' WOW! It was certainly okay with me! Mrs. came rushing out of the kitchen and cried 'I thought I recognized that voice, Hallo Shezza, come in out of the cold. Let her in, Mr. it's not a canvasser, its Shezza!'

When she floated in and clapped eyes on me, Shezza's smile lit up the room like a ray of sunshine down a coal mine. 'Hallo little fellow, she whispered, I would like us to be friends.' Rufus popped out from behind the sofa, hoping to stick his snout in and get a pat on the head from her until I snarled at him. *'Back off Buster, this one's mine!!'* She knelt down and offered her hand to me so I rubbed my head against it and made all the right purring noises that showed I was happy to be her friend. After cuddling up to her for a while, I was smitten, ready to go right now without packing. A short while ago I was planning to bite her ankles. Now I was ready to follow her to the ends of the earth.

After a while Shezza was having tea and biscuits with Mr. and Mrs. and discussing my possible move. Ooh, I can hardly wait. They were saying that I could still see Mr. and Mrs. If I wanted to from time to time and that's fine with me. They took me home when I was abandoned and I owe them for that. But I will be quite happy to keep out of Rufus's way and being his fall guy.

FIVE.

MARCH 2014. *New Horizons.*

And so it came to pass, the day that Shezza brought a cage for me to travel in, which would protect me from grizzly bears, mountain lions or wolves on our intrepid journey through the treacherous frozen wastelands to reach Shezza's home… Actually it's just around the corner about three streets away but it sounds good and it *was* chilly. Mr. and Mrs. waved us off and we made our way down the street. Even Rufus came to the door, probably wondering who he could blame for his future misdeeds. Mr. was grumbling to Mrs. about his missing Senna tablets. 'I'm sure I had twice that amount last night, and now there appears to be half of them missing.' 'Well I haven't had them, said Mrs. 'my bowel is fine thank you, I have no idea where they might have gone.' *'Well I have,' I whispered under my breath, 'try Rufus's biscuit box, mixed in nicely. They should keep him on the go for a while.'*

Battling against all odds with grim determination, we finally reached our destination safely, five minutes later.

27

Shezza lives in a flat above a chip shop and as we headed for the stairs at the side of the building, my nose was assailed with the smell of fish frying, a wonderful aroma to any cat. 'I'm going to like it here,' I thought. As we ascended the stairs I caught a glimpse of bins in the chippy yard. That will be my first place to investigate when Shezza lets me out. I also noticed two huge seagulls perched on a rooftop quite close to where we were heading. Then the unthinkable happened. Shezza smiled and waved at them! Surely they can't be friends of hers? There's an unwritten law concerning seagulls and humans and definitely cats. I was brought up to believe that we were sworn enemies. 'Yoo hoo,' shouts Shezza, 'I'm home.' The gulls started squawking at her, begging for food. 'I've got some bits for you as soon as I can get inside.' The gulls squawked some more in anticipation. 'By the way,' she said, holding my carry cage aloft so that the gulls could see me, 'this is Riley Anthony. He might be staying with us if he settles down here.' 'Now Riley,' she continued, 'say hallo to Belinda and Grace.' The gulls squawked hallo at me and I did my impression of Hannibal Lector through the bars at them trying to look fierce. The pair of them fell about, laughing.

When we were finally inside I took my time exploring the place. Quite a nice pad on the whole with a large double bed which must be where I was expected to rest my weary head at night. For daytime snoozing there were various cozy places on the sofa or armchairs with no interference from a dog called Rufus. Things were looking promising but first I had to lay down my own ground rules, namely, I like feather pillows, eat only the finest cuts of fish, and roast beef or chicken. Not TURKEY, definitely, NOT TURKEY! I have to be allowed out on request, and non-disturbed sleeping time for me is anytime between midday and midnight. After that it's 'game on.' Oh yes, and I don't take baths on any day that ends in 'ay.' Once we get these minor things sorted I should settle in just fine.

SIX.

April 2014. *Healthy diets don't agree with me.*

Four weeks have passed and I have kept my nose clean and done my level best to get used to Shezza's quirky ways. Okay, so feather pillows are out because apparently they make her sneeze. I have to share my double bed with her until she can afford one for herself and as for the food, let's just say that I am on some kind of starvation diet, thought up by a fiendish vet and disguised as being healthy.

Shezza is out most of the day working part time in a café during the mornings and at a fish emporium in the evenings. There is a patio at the entrance to the flat with a locked gate to the stairs. She thinks it's a safe enclosure for me with a strong fence on two sides and a parapet wall overlooking the Chip shop yard at the far end. If I stand on the wall I can see the bins in the yard below. What's more, I can smell waste fish in the bins.

I know it won't help my street cred, but Belinda and Grace are the first seagulls I have ever made friends with. Shezza feeds them tidbits and in return they deter other gulls from 'dive bombing' her washing. They showed me the easiest way down to the bins, but flap my paws like a windmill and I still can't get lift off. I found my own way eventually. Scrabbling down to a small roof gets me halfway, and then it's an easy leap to the nearest bin. As long as Shezza doesn't spot me down here it should be okay. She keeps me on a healthy diet so I don't want her knowing about my 'extras' from the chippy.

Belinda and Grace make a good team along with myself. We work well together down in the chippy yard. Me using my superior strength to hold up the bin lids while they swoop in and grab any waste fish they can find. We then share the proceeds and everybody's happy. It was going quite well until a very wet day when the heavy lid slipped through my paws. Belinda didn't take too kindly to being plunged into darkness in a metal dungeon. She started tapping out frantic Morse code with her beak on the sides, which loosely translated was, er, best not translated. I dried my paws on Grace's feathers as quickly as I could and got Belinda out. After that scare we all agreed to be more careful in future. The next time I lifted a bin lid Grace flew in with a piece of driftwood from the beach and wedged the lid open. This meant we could take our time and was much safer. But we got complacent and forgot to remove it one day causing Chippy John to pause and scratch his head when he came out to dump waste. A few days later, disaster! All the lids had a heavy weight placed on them that even I with my supa dupa strength couldn't shift. Just to add more misery on the day, Shezza had booked me a visit to Victor the vet where I failed miserably on the scales having gained a little weight. 'You must be feeding him too much, try cutting down on his portions' ordered Victor. This was not what I wanted to hear. I like my food and plenty of it. New food strategy had to be found and while discussing it with Belinda and Grace I brought up the option of the harbour gutting sheds and the overflowing bins behind them. They stared at me as if I was mad then looked at each other and shook their heads. 'We try to avoid that place unless we are really desperate,' whispered Belinda, as if afraid someone might overhear us.

'It's not just Jellybone Frazer and his gang,' added Grace, 'There are some vicious gulls out there from foreign ports. They follow the trawlers in.'

'There was a whisper,' began Belinda, before being interrupted by Grace.

'Don't tell him, you will frighten him!'

'Don't tell me what? You have to tell me now' I pleaded.

'He should be warned, so that he can avoid the danger,' Belinda implored of Grace.

'Okay then, go ahead, I suppose forewarned is forearmed' admitted Grace. Before they spoke I said 'look, if this is about Jellybone Frazer I think he's just a big overgrown bully. I have dealt with him before, and his sidekicks. They are just a bunch of feral fleabags who like to throw their weight around. Anyway, if I want to avoid them I can take a short cut across the harbour by leaping from boat to boat. I don't mind if I fall in the sea. I can swim so that's not a problem. Jelly and his gang guard the road entrance to the sheds. I can cut around behind them.' They both shook their heads from side to side. 'It's not Jellybone or his gang,' Belinda whispered. 'It's, it's'…her voice trailed off.

'Oh do spit it out,' Grace yelled, 'if you must know its Afghan Abdul, the fiercest seagull around here. You can usually see him sharpening his beak on the harbour wall. They say that his favourite meal is diced cat tail! And he's teamed up with Jellybone for a share of the fish waste.' 'Oooohh,' I shivered, 'I'm quite fond of my tail, I've had it since I was little and I don't want to lose it or cross swords with him if I can help it.'

'Then stay away from the gutting sheds' they begged. 'We will bring you any spare fish we find.' After thanking them I thought, I have to get more grub from somewhere. Shezzas healthy diet is a little too healthy for my liking.

SEVEN.

MAY 2014. *I'm as thin as a racing snake*

Another four weeks have passed and Shezzas lean mean healthy diet is beginning to bite into my fat reserves. Victor the vet was ecstatic when I floated onto the scales. I was hoping he would recommend building me up with a heavier diet, but the Puddinhead cried 'Excellent Shezza, keep up the good work and we will soon have him in shape.' *In shape? In shape? I look like a herring bone already. This cannot go on.* I resolved there and then that it was high time I paid a visit to the harbour gutting sheds and filled my belly. Afghan Abdul and Jellybone's mob could go take a running jump. I was feeling fed up and very hungry.

It's the middle of May. Lots of sunshine and a warm breeze are making it a pleasure to be out and about, mingling with holidaymakers, who always seem to have some kind of food to share, with a hungry looking cat whose ribs are sticking out. Shezza has allowed me to follow her further afield while I get used to the area. We go as far as a little park cum gardens not too far away. The gardens are a great place for me to explore and a lovely gardener called George, rakes the soil under the bushes to a fine tilth so that it's not too rough on my backside when I do my ablutions. He comes along later and rakes it all in again ready for tomorrow. He must really like his work because he smiles a lot while he's raking, although sometimes his smile looks a bit like a grimace. Maybe his boots are rubbing his toes.

Shezza thinks that the park is as far as I go, but she forgets that in the past I had the run of the harbour and the beaches. I have spent many happy days along Brid seafront rubbing shoulders, well, ankles actually, with cheery holidaymakers as they soaked up the relaxing atmosphere of this place. Everything they could wish for is right here on the doorstep. From a stately home on Northside, to a funfair at central, and the Spa theatre on Southside, where lots of famous stars are proud to perform. The Harbour is always a hive of activity, with fishing boats and pleasure craft. A boat trip around the Bay is so refreshing, and they don't charge for cats. There are lots of benches along the Promenade where people will sit to watch the world go by, and eat their sandwiches, sharing them happily with a friendly cat like me. But the beaches are my favourite place. Miles of clean golden sand, raked over every day by our local council, who, in their infinite wisdom have deemed that not one scrap of today's litter will see the light of tomorrows dawn. It's the same with the emptying of the litter bins around Town which starts at some unearthly hour and wakes me up most mornings long before I want to rise. Our local MP, Clifton Bladderhead is so intent on cleanliness that I wouldn't be surprised to see Sam the street sweeper polishing manhole covers with 'Brasso' in the near future.

But, back to those glorious beaches where I can stroll from one family to another and join in a picnic or two. I love nothing better, on a hot day than running up and down to the water's edge with the kids and splashing around. They think it strange to find a cat that is not afraid to paddle, but I had a bad experience with water when I was little and the only way I got over it was by watching how other people enjoyed the water and introducing myself back to it slowly. Now I think nothing of getting soaked, then curling up in a deckchair and drying out in the sun. I find that when the lunch boxes and hampers come out the best thing to do is line up with the other children and wait my turn. It's amazing how parents don't count how many children they are feeding. Dressed Crab or Potted Shrimps are placed in front of me with a remark like 'young un needs his hair cuttin' and I just enjoy it. But since I moved in with Shezza I don't get down there so often. She thinks I might get lost. There's not much chance of that.

EIGHT.

JUNE2014.   *D. Day approaches.*

I've had enough of waiting. I can put it off no longer. All I can think about day and night is a visit to the harbour gutting sheds and filling this great empty space in my stomach. I'm even dreaming about it every time I close my eyes. It's alright for Victor the Vet. He must be getting more than a fair share judging by his waistline, while I look like I've been attacked by a school of starving Piranha's. I can see bones that I never knew I had. But Victor is happy, his assistant with the cold hands is happy, and Shezza is happy. They all agree that I am at my ideal weight. *Ideal weight?* Ideal for whom, may I ask?   I'm not a whippet I'm a cat, and we are traditionally fat. Well, slightly overweight at least. No, I'm afraid that the time has come to take myself down to the harbour and check out the facilities. Maybe Jelly's mob has moved on and things are quieter down there, after all, it is quite a while since I last visited the sheds.

Today is the day. I have laid awake half the night listening to what I thought might be trains rumbling past until I realized that it was actually my stomach. There is so much gas in there that I could inflate a hot air balloon all by myself. I tried to leave at the same time as Shezza set out for work but she shut me in. 'You have a nice rest today Riley, you've been out a lot lately, keep an eye on the flat for me and I'll bring you a nice treat home.' *Treat?* What, like that seaweed and Senna biscuit you gave me yesterday? No thanks, from now on I'll find my own treats!

Racing upstairs and forcing myself out of the bedroom window as fast as a burglar with a Rottweiler on his backside, I scrambled down the drainpipe to freedom. Hitting the street in S.A.S. mode I kept Shezza in sight and followed her stealthily, keeping to shadowy shop doorways. She bade a cheery 'Good Morning' to lots of people along the way and never looked back once. Lingering in the entrance to Swindell and Robb, the estate agents, I watched her walk the last few steps and into the café to start her shift. Still keeping a low profile, I made my way toward the Harbour and almost ended up in Scarborough General instead. Looking right, left, then right again and putting one paw forward to cross a busy pavement, I was almost mown down by 'Ferrari Fred' on his mobility scooter. The one with the go faster stripes and imitation chrome exhaust. He seems to think he's taking part in a Grand Prix. Sweeping along the pavement scaring old ladies witless, by shouting 'get out of my way, the accelerator's jammed!' But if you follow him, you will find that he just wants to be first in the Post Office queue, in case the money runs out before he claims his pension. There's nothing wrong with his legs either. The mobility scooter is just a lot cheaper to run than a car, and easier to park.

Taking a deep breath to clear my head, I tried to concentrate on the job in hand. Finally arriving at the Harbour and settling down across the road, I carried out surveillance of the entrance. No sign of Jelly or his crew meant that it was safer for me to get closer. There were a number of people fishing with rod and line over the sea wall so I weaved my way through them while checking their baskets to see if there was any spare fish on offer. Being out of luck, I carried on along the road carefully, finding it strangely quiet. Ahead of me lay a battered Trawler anchored up to the dockside. It gave no clue to where it was from as the whole structure was a mishmash of rust and flaking paint obliterating its details. White and rust, grey and rust, plus rust and rust. It had certainly seen better days. On the bow I could just make out the words 'Red Star'. It was evidently a work horse judging by the baskets of fish being unloaded from its hold and disappearing into the gutting sheds. It suddenly dawned on me that Jelly and Co. could be reaping the benefits of the waste around the back. A furtive glance over the wall proved this to be right. I would have to wait until they filled up and fell asleep. Then I could go in and fill me up. I could hardly wait.

In the past when I have visited here, my favourite place to hide until the coast is clear is under the metal staircase that runs down the side of the sheds. To reach it I have to cross a gap in the wall where I could be spotted. So it means waiting until the road is absolutely clear and making a dash for it. If Jelly sees me it will be goodbye fish and hello fists. What I really needed now was Grace or Belinda to fly overhead and carry out a recce. But Grace told me last night that she would be visiting her poorly Auntie Joyce up at the bird sanctuary on Bempton Cliffs and taking Belinda with her. Those two are inseparable. I have never seen a happier pair of girls, and if any chaps stick their nose in, they get short shrift. As for Auntie Joyce, apparently she ate some dodgy oysters. Grace said that she should know better at her age. This leaves me on my own here, despite the pair of them warning me not to venture down alone. But I just had to respond to the call of the wild, and my growling gut.

Flattening myself against the wall where it ended, and satisfied that the 'undead' all had their heads in the bins, I tensed like a coiled spring ready to cross the gap to the safety of the dark underside of the stairwell. Once again I slip into commando mode. Deep breath, exhale slowly. One last glance, left and right. Eyes front, concentrating on the target. Deep breath in again, holding it steady and, STOP! Stay absolutely still. Something is happening, under the stairs, in the gloom. Someone must be in my hidey hole. I cannot believe my eyes, or what I am seeing. A small piece of fish was tossed out of the shadows and into the open. After a few seconds, a large rat emerged from a hole in a cracked drainpipe at the side of the stairs. The rat cautiously sniffed the air, looked around then moved toward the fish. Just as it reached it, a blurry shape of pink and grey appeared at lightning speed, grabbed the rat, flung it far out over the sea wall and disappeared under the stair again before I could make out just what it was. This scenario was repeated three times before one of the rats escaped by the skin of its teeth, and then ran blindly into me. I clutched him, gave his head a little knock to daze him and threw him back toward the stair. The pink blur caught him before he hit the ground and sent him over the wall to join the others. It was an automatic reflex on my part but now I had given my position away and whatever it was under the stair was probably watching me.

Waiting with bated breath, the sweat began to trickle down my whiskers making me want to sneeze. I sensed movement in the shadows, and my heart almost stopped. It began to emerge into daylight but neither my eyes nor brain could make sense of it. I caught a glimpse of red, which seemed to be some kind of hat or turban. Below the hat were two large, no, extra-large red eyes looking in different directions at the same time. Circling like Radar dishes on a ship. The head that they were attached to began to move from side to side while the orbs circled. My eyes were glued to it and the whole motion was making me feel dizzy. When it focused onto me, my knees went weak and I forgot to breathe. I wanted to flee but was rooted to the spot. As the main body of it moved toward me I saw a big catlike shape, devoid of fur, with pink blotchy skin and little tufts of hair, sprouting in patches. Strangest of all, it appeared to be wearing a skirt and boots to match the hat. I didn't feel well at all. I thought that I must be suffering from some kind of illusion. As it got closer, I just had time to wonder if this was the great Alopecia monster my mother threatened me with when I wouldn't be a good kitten and do my grooming, then I flaked out.

NINE.

JUNE 2014.   *LYDIA.*

I don't know how long I was unconscious, drifting along in a haze of cod liver oil odours. As I slowly surfaced, the smell got stronger. Forcing one eye open I found *IT* standing over me breathing garlic and diesel fumes in my face while dabbing my head with a piece of wet cod. I tried to make sense of this creature before me but my brain was aching. I have never before, come across a big bald hairless *cat?* Wearing a red hat, with matching skirt and boots. I concluded that I must have concussion. Trying to focus my brain again proved fruitless. It was wallowing in shock and quite content to stay there. Breathing in deeply, with my heart thumping like a sledgehammer, I finally managed to mutter 'who are you? What are you? Do you come in peace?'

In a strange accent it said 'vot I ams and oo I ams, zis yoo vish to know Pushkin? Yes? No?'
I managed 'er, um, er yes, I think.'
It pointed toward the rusting hulk anchored up.
'I am zer sheeps cat. My verk eez to reed zer sheep of rats.' I was looking at it blankly so it continued 'I verk on many sheeps all over zer North Zea. I theenk I am zer only female to do zo. Sheeps cat are usually male, but I am beeg and stronger zan most of zem.'

47

'You are a cat? And female?' I blurted out, then wished I hadn't and bit my tongue. This was the largest and strangest looking feline that I had ever come across and I didn't want to upset *it, her, whatever.* Don't get me wrong, I have been out with some weird specimens in my time, usually making up a foursome for a friend. Donkeys and goats I can abide, but this one was different, with a capital diff. It looked like a cat, yes, albeit oversized and hairless. It was wearing a red turban, yes, with a matching skirt, yes, and matching boots, yes. But as for female I wasn't too sure. Maybe a sheepdog in drag?

It, her, whatever, must have been reading my thoughts. It spoke ' Yoo vant to inzult me Pushkin, or be my friend?' I took a deep breath but before I could speak it continued 'Theenk carefully before you answer me, Pushkin Prettyboy.'

I wasn't too sure about the name it had given me. Was I really that good looking? Then again, who am I to argue? It obviously had good taste.

Discretion being my middle name, I answered 'of course I don't want to insult you and I really would like to make your acquaintance, er, um, er, young lady.' This seemed to please her, thank god. I had just noticed that her paws were almost the same size as my head.

'Then tell me Pushkin Prettyboy, vot iz yoor name?'
'Riley Anthony,' I replied, 'I live here.'

She drew herself up to her full height, leaving her chest level with my nose. I tried standing on tiptoe but it didn't make much difference.

'Yoo are very fortunate, Rylee Anzony, to be making zer acquaintance of a famous zeafaring cat like me.' She spread her arms wide and with a flourish announced 'I am Lydiarnavich Gregorina Lubyanska, but yoo can call me Lydiarnavich Gregorina for short, okay? Pushkin Prettyboy?'

I must admit to being a little tongue tied for a second or two. 'Er, um, are you kidding me?'

'I never keed anyones, I am how yoo zay ? All up front and een yoor face.'

'You can say that again,' I muttered, stepping back, 'kindly keep your chest under control. You nearly poked my eye out then.'

'Vots that yoo zay pushkin?'

'I said how would it be if I just call you Lydia? It would be easier for me to remember.'

She considered this for a while then said 'Okay Rylee, vee vill leave it at zat for now. Zo, vot do yoo do in zis Breedlinton? Yoo maybe verk in butcher shop ver zer eez lots of meat?' I shook my head. She looked disappointed. 'Or in soopermarket on meat counter? I shook my head again. She rolled her eyes, the big gogglyy orbs. 'Do yoo verk near any kind of meat?'

'Er, I don't verk, I mean work, actually. But I can get you food, if you want some.'

'Vill zis food be meat?'

'It could well be,' I replied.

'Zen vot are ve vaiting for?' And with that, she slipped her arm in mine and set off down the Harbour road.

'Wait a minute,' I said, 'I came here for some scraps from the gutting shed waste bins.' She performed a quick about turn and led me back to the stairwell where she had been hiding. Thrusting her paw into the darkness, she pulled out a huge piece of cod and passed it to me. 'Thank you, I gasped, thank you very much.'

'Yoo arr most velcome Rilee Anzony, eet it up.' And that's just what I did. Made a pig of myself, in front of my new found friend. But she didn't seem to mind. I offered her some but she declined, *thank goodness,* saying that she was 'seek of feesh, day in, day out.' It tasted so good I wouldn't mind getting sick of it at least three times a week.

While I was eating, she told me that the ship had been heading for the port of Hull but had developed engine trouble and crawled into the nearest safe harbour, at Bridlington. The engineer had announced that repairs would take at least three days and the Captain had granted most of the crew shore leave.

'Does that include the ships cat?' I enquired.

'Az long az I keep watch on zer rats, I am free to come and go' was her reply.

'In that case let's go, and I will introduce you to some of my friends.' I could hardly wait to see the look on their faces when I showed up with her. Engrossed in deciding where to take her first and completely forgetting about Jelly and co. we set off down the Harbour road. We were almost halfway along when I recognized the figures blocking the way forward. Jellybone Frazer is notorious for his cruelty to other cats. He is a big overweight slug of a ginger tom, with a face like a three day old curry and a smile like a constipated crocodile. He gets his kicks from making others suffer. I didn't know the two sidekicks with him but they were doing their best to look mean under the guidance off their bullying boss. They spread out and stood tall, puffing out their chests. Each of them had a short length of rusty chain which they swung menacingly. Jelly was deciding whether to chew on his chain, like a pacifier, or part my hair with it. I could see in his eyes that he had chosen the latter and intended to change my mullet into a skinhead with a few quick slashes.

He finally spoke. 'You have been warned before about coming down here without my permission Riley, and taking our food.' The chain was twirling above his head now. 'Okay Riley boy, come and get your punishment.' His eyes suddenly shifted to Lydia who had been standing behind me but had now stepped forward. 'Who's your freaky friend? Or should I say what's your freaky friend? Does it want its features rearranging too?'

Lydia turned to me, her right eyebrow raised in question. I tried to send a silent message to her brain. *Please don't call me Pushkin in front of these idiots. Aghhh too late. Lydia was already speaking.* 'If yoo don't take back what yoo just zaid and clear away, my friend Pushkin Prettyboy vill make yoo very zorry.' Complete silence followed for a few seconds then hoots of laughter echoed around the harbour.

'Puskin Prettyboy? HAH HAH HAH!' I thought Jelly and his boys would crack a rib or two, they laughed so hard, falling about slapping each other on the back and giggling. My reputation would be shot after this, so although I try to avoid confrontation where possible, this time I had to do something. *'Go straight for Jelly,'* I told myself and measured the distance between us, ready to pounce. Before I could move, a blur of red and pink sped from my side like an Exocet rocket and launched into them, paws flailing like a walrus having a fit while practicing hand jive. Ten seconds later, all three of them were over the seawall and learning to swim the hard way.

Lydia straightened her hat, dusted her paws and said 'Zat has geeve me appetite Pushkin. Show me to zis macdoogals verr I can eat vot eez not feesh.'

'Okay, I replied, but I'm not sure if it's meat either.' Once again we set of toward the main road. Glancing over the sea wall I noticed Jelly being helped onto the beach by one of his cronies. The third one was nowhere to be seen. Looking back to where they went over, I could see him clinging to the sea wall and slipping under as waves broke over his head. Obviously a non-swimmer, he was calling for help from his mates but they just slunk off up the beach. 'It's no use Lydia, I can't leave him there, he might drown,' I gasped. Running back along the top of the sea wall I performed the perfect swallow dive with double pike as I dove into space and entered the water seamlessly. *Actually I slipped in something dubious on the wall but I made it look good, although I did hit the water like an elephant dropping down a lift shaft.* Spreading my arms and legs helped me to float on the water. Grabbing him unceremoniously by his tail then swimming sidestroke and kicking strongly, we were on the beach in no time at all. He coughed and spluttered a lot until he got his breath back. Then, as I waited for a 'thank you' he took a bite at my tail and ran off. Lydia strolled down the beach to join me as I dried out in the warm afternoon sun. 'Yoo are beeg softee, Rylee, wiz heart of gold, but how long must I vait for my deener?' We headed for the alley at the rear of the nearest Restaurant. Where there are waste bins, there will be food. There will also be cats but I know most of them. At the first place, we came across an old friend of mine, Limpalong Lennie. He's a black cat with one eye, one ear, one missing leg and only half a tail. 'Eez zat eez real name? Lydia whispered.

'No, I replied, his real name is Lucky but nobody calls him that anymore.' Lucky had a fright when he clapped his eye on Lydia but settled down when he saw me and I introduced her to him and told him that she was hungry. Lucky pointed at the bins. 'First one is fish.' Lydia grimaced. 'Second one is burgers.' This put a smile on Lydia's chops and she dove straight in.

'May I? She asked.

'Be my guest,' replied Lucky, 'any friend of Riley's is always welcome here. There's plenty to go round' he added, as Lydia made herself a double triple burger stack. While she was busy in the bin he turned to me and stated 'You have been around here with some strange looking, er, companions Riley, but this one definitely takes the biscuit, or burgers, so to speak.'

'I have to agree with you Lucky, but you can't judge a book by its cover, as my old granny used to say. And this one is growing on me.'

Growing on you? I thought you said that you've only known her for five minutes.'

'That's true but I think she's got something special.'

He looked over at Lydia and whispered 'yes and she needs it looking at.'

When Lydia had eaten enough 'meat' to last her the afternoon I suggested a walk along the prom.

'I vud razzer look at shops first' she replied. *HUH, typical woman I thought.* So we bade farewell to Lucky, thanked him again for the food and hit the high street, trailing from shop to shop gazing into every window until I realized that we were next to the cafe where Shezza works 'Yikes!' She thinks I'm safely locked up at home and here I am outside her workplace getting more than a few strange glances from passersby because of my odd looking companion. 'Time we moved on Lydia, Shezza finishes work soon and I need to be home before her.' Guiding her away from the café and back toward the seafront took us past 'Lyons' florist. I used to step out with 'Dandy,' a pretty Persian living there. She always smelled sweet but her temper was on the sour side. She was on the doorstep as we strolled past. Her eyes were fixated on Lydia. When Lydia stared back then rolled her large eyes in different directions at the same time, Dandy stepped back inside, startled.

'Friend of yoors?' Lydia asked.

'Er, an old family friend,' I replied.

'Liar,' she said, 'vy did yoo part from her?'

'She wanted me to move into the flower shop with her. Called me a weed when I turned her down.'

We continued left onto the promenade and strolled along in the late afternoon sun. Pensioners sat along the front gazing out to sea, eating their sandwiches and pouring stewed tea from big metal flasks. One or two of them shared a few bits with us. Like me, I think they were fascinated by this overgrown cross eyed cat dressed in red co-ordinates. 'Vell Rylee, I theenk eet eez time I report back to sheep. Rats vill be cominz back on board if I am not zerr to stop zem.'

'Okay Lydia, I have to get back myself. Will I see you tomorrow?'

'Zat vud be nice if yoo can come down to zer harbour.'

'I'll do my best Lydia, bye.'

What I earlier thought of as a goggle eyed monster was turning out to be the nicest of cats. She wasn't forthcoming about the missing fur or the wearing of clothes but maybe I will ask her tomorrow. I watched her head back down the prom, and then I high tailed it back home. It was much harder getting up the drainpipe and in through the window but I made it with seconds to spare as I heard Shezzas key turn in the lock. Flinging myself onto the sofa and shutting my eyes tight, I snored a little until Shezza stroked my head. A great yawn from me convinced her that I hadn't budged since she had left this morning. 'Oh you are a dozy cat Riley, let's go outside and get some fresh air. I've been cooped up in the café all day just like you've been cooped up in here.' I nodded meekly and followed her outside. Belinda and Grace were just returning from an afternoon foraging down at the harbour after spending the morning with poorly auntie Joyce up at Bempton. Belinda tipped me a sly wink and Grace tapped the side of her beak in a 'mums the word' fashion. They must have seen me with Lydia. I couldn't wait to get to bed. It had been a hectic day, but Shezza wanted to play. She kept throwing my ball and I had to chase it and look as if I was enjoying myself. When we did finally settle down indoors I had time to think about my new found friend and wondered where her fur had gone. I must ask her tomorrow but in a way so as not to upset her, after all, her paws are the size of dinner plates.

TEN.

JUNE2014.   *A quiet Day?*

I behaved like a little angel that night. I didn't jump onto the bed in the early hours waking Shezza like I usually did when I'd had enough sleep. I was so tired that I stayed on the sofa all night, snoring my whiskers off. Shezza had a good sleep and came downstairs looking for me. 'Morning Riley, my my, you have had a good sleep. Indoors all of yesterday and you've been quiet all night. I'm working all day today so I think for a change perhaps you can stay out, after a good breakfast of course, if that's okay with you. The fresh air will do you good.' I could hardly believe my luck and gave Shezza lots of attention while she got ready for work. After a hearty breakfast of stale ships biscuit and weevils, (that's what my latest diet tastes like) I was good to go. Shezza opened the door to the patio and left me a bowl of water and more hardtack in case I got peckish. I would have to dump it in a bin somewhere so that she would think I had eaten it. I bade farewell to Shezza and made my way down to my favourite little park and my toilet facilities. George the gardener had been hard at work so the soil was finely sifted. He had placed a few plants here and there which I thought was really nice of him. To make my toilet arca so attractive was real dedication on his part. After making good use of it to show my appreciation, I set off toward the harbour.

Approaching the harbour entrance with caution I stayed on the opposite side of the road and waited for a while to make sure the coast was clear. It had the makings of a fine day with a clear blue sky and a heat haze shimmering toward the horizon. No sign of Jellybone left me relaxed but also a little bit apprehensive. Lydia's ship was rising and falling with the swell and my heart started to follow suit as she sashayed down the gangplank. She caught site of me and waved. I waved back and waited for a gap in the traffic so that I could cross over the road. I managed it just before a group of bikers cruised by. She looked pretty as a picture with matching hat, skirt and boots. Today's colour scheme was powder blue. She blended in with the sky and the sea behind her. Belinda and Grace appeared suddenly, flapping furiously, as they tried to catch my attention. 'He's back!' They both yelled, 'Jelly's friend, Afghan Abdul!'   Lydia was halfway along the harbour road and I was at the entrance. Glancing all around I felt reassured when I found no sign of Jellybone or his cronies, and the only gulls flapping around were my friends. A distance of twenty yards separated us when Belinda and Grace started squawking. 'He's here! Over there!' I looked to my right toward the south beach and saw a huge bird coming in fast from the sea. As it drew nearer it became obvious that it was very large. It skimmed across the waves and then the sand staying low. It was heading straight for the harbour wall but at the last possible moment it swerved up and over the wall. My heart stood still as its intentions became clear. Lydia had her eyes fixed on me as I waved furiously to warn her. The bird struck her on the side of the head at speed and she fell to the ground. Her pretty little hat rolled over the harbour edge and dropped into the oily water. I began to run toward Lydia when the gull landed between us. *Did I say gull?* This monster looked more like a Pterodactyl. His cruel beak was the longest I have seen and razor sharp by the look of it. He faced me, spreading his wings wide then scraped his beak along the top of the seawall. I think it produced sparks. He was trying to scare me. It worked. 'Stay back Riley cat or I will turn you into a colander,' he hissed. With a beak like that it wouldn't take long. I stood still and glanced around, searching for help but none was forthcoming. I spotted Jelly and his miserable cronies down on the beach, observing from a distance and staying out of the way. This was obviously a set up by them.

Abdul turned his back to me, confident that I was too petrified to move. He was almost right, *almost.* Turning his attention to Lydia, who by know was up on one elbow still looking dazed, he hissed 'So, Rat cat, we meet again! You refused me food when I came onto your ship and now I have good friend Jellybone who gives me all the fish I want. He asks me for favour to teach you a lesson.'

Lydia shook her head. 'I deedn't refuse yoo food. Yoo *demanded* it. All yoo had to do vas zay please and I vud have geeve yoo feesh.'

'The great Abdul does not beg from female! I snap my beak and they give whatever I want. When I have finished with you, you also will bow to my command!'

'Een yoor dreems Featherhead! Ven I get my hands on yoor scrawny neck, I vill turn yoo into corkscrew!' Lydia struggled to her feet but I could see that she was still quite groggy. That knock on the head and fall onto the cobbles had left her winded. Looking around desperately I found the road behind me was empty all the way back to the harbour entrance. Empty except for a litter bin, courtesy of our clean up councilor, Clifton Bladderhead. OH! *Suddenly I love that man!* Leaving Lydia at the mercy of Abdul and dashing back to the bin, I grabbed the inner liner which is quite heavy metal, tipping the contents onto the floor (*Sorry councillor)* as I ran back. Abdul was strutting about and striking out at Lydia. The sun glinted on his evil looking beak as he raised it high, preparing to strike down at her where she lay. My plan, well, I didn't actually have one. I was intending to rush straight into him with the bin and see what happened. It didn't happen. Somehow, in my haste, I managed to trip over my tail, fall flat on my face and lose my grip on the bin. It sailed through the air in a perfect arc and seemed to hover before dropping down over Abduls head, pinning his wings to his sides with a sickening scrunch and breaking off the end of his beak. Only his feet were visible as he yelled and screamed in a tinny echoey voice. Lydia was beaming. 'Bravo Rylee, perfect aim. I deedn't know yoo were zo good.'

Neither did I. 'I er, I used to train with a basketball team' was all I could think of on the spur of the moment. Abdul was well and truly stuck in the bin for the time being but we needed somewhere safe to put him. He was walking into the harbour wall and falling over, much to the amusement of Belinda and Grace who had been hovering around. We tipped him on his side and rolled him over the cobbles all the way back to the main road and the ramp which runs down to the beach. With one final heave we sent him helter skelter down to the sand where Jellybone and friends were expecting a much different outcome. Lydia stepped forward raising her paw at Jelly. He turned and fled as fast as his furry legs would carry him.

Belinda flew over with Lydia's powder blue hat after fishing it out of the harbour. It was more powder brown now but Grace flew out with it and rinsed it in the sea. 'It should soon dry out,' she said.

I turned to Lydia 'that was a scary start to the day. let's hope that things calm down now.' We ambled along the seafront until we came to the main car park. Motorcyclists were gathering and checking out each bike that came in. 'You okay Lydia?' I queried.

'Yez I am fine now,' she smiled. 'Do zees bikerz come often to here?'

'Yes, they have meetings in Whitby and Scarborough but those in the know make their way here for the atmosphere.'

' Vud yoo like to ride motorbike Rylee?'

' Er, well, yes, I fancy myself on a 'DuCATTI' actually.' She laughed at that and said ' yoo vud look good in lezzers Rylee.'

I shook my head, 'I'm not too sure about the leathers Lydia, the smell reminds me of some of my old relatives.'

Lots of people were gathering to look at the shiny motorcycles and some people were eating snacks. One such person was sharing a ham sandwich with Lydia when I turned to look for her. 'What a big smart looking cat you are. My Riley would love to meet you, I'm sure.' AAAGGHH! It was Shezza, out on her lunch break. I stood quite still and tried to look like a pannier saddlebag, but when I dared to glance at Shezza, she was already staring at me. She looked shocked, surprised and even speechless all at once, which is a first for Shezza. I enjoyed the silence. It didn't last long. 'What the heck are you doing down here? I didn't think you went further than the park! People came into the café yesterday and said they had seen an odd couple outside, but I thought that you were in the flat all day so it couldn't be you, and, OH MY GAWD! It was you wasn't it? How did you get out, and back in again? I hung my head and looked sad, that usually works. It did. 'It's a good job you've found a friend to watch out for you.' Shezza gave the last of her sandwich to Lydia. Lydia passed half to me. 'My, you are good friends.' Lydia allowed Shezza to stroke her. 'You've lost some of your fur but it will soon grow back if you treat it, she smiled, I can get something from the vet for you, if you like, then you won't need to dress to cover the thin parts.' She glanced at her watch. 'Got to go Riley, but bring your friend for tea, see you later.' Shezza set off back to work and Lydia waved after her. 'Vot a nice lady, yoo are very fortunate Rylee.'

'I know Lydia, it's my natural charm that wows her.' That set her off laughing, which was nice. I liked it when she laughed. We visited Limpalong Lennie again and stashed a couple of burgers in a plastic bag. 'Thanks again Lennie, I owe you.' Lennie waved us away. 'Have a nice day, you two.'

We ambled along North beach where there are lots of small secluded gardens with benches at the side of the promenade. The Sun was high and we needed a rest after the morning activity. Settling on the lush grass surrounded by sweet smelling flowers, we attacked the burgers. Lydia turned to me. I could see a question in her big goggly eyes. I could also see my reflection so I took the opportunity to straighten my hair and smooth my whiskers.

Finally she spoke. 'Vee only met yesterday and I know so leetle about you.'

'Like what? Ask away.'

'Like verr yoo come from, av yoo got bruzzerz and seesterz? But most of all I vish to know ver yoo learned to svim, like when you rescue zee cat from zer harbour yesterday.' I relaxed, and lay back with my paws behind my head for a pillow, deep in thought. 'I was born here Lydia, and I can just about remember other kittens snuggled up around me, but I was snatched away from them by a young man. He said he would teach me to swim. After putting me into a plastic bag, he threw me over the harbour wall and shouted 'get out of that if you can, Riley.' Lydia gasped and shook her head. I continued 'my little claws were very sharp and I managed to tear the bag open. After some frantic splashing around, the tide carried me onto the beach. I didn't like the cold water much and I thought that he would be proud of me when I caught up with him but he seemed to be annoyed. I was hoping he would take me back to the other kittens but he said that I needed a harder test.' I paused for a moment to recollect my memory of that day. It was a recurring nightmare that woke me up many a night afterwards. Lydia was looking at me expectantly so I continued. 'He took me up to Flamborough Head and this time he put me into a large black dustbin sack. After swinging me around his head a few times he flung me out into space. It was very dark in that sack and I didn't like the falling sensation at all. When I hit the water, the impact almost knocked me senseless.' Lydia gasped again as I carried on, 'I scrabbled and clawed at the thick plastic but only managed to make a few holes in it which allowed the water to seep in. And that's where I learned to swim. Inside that sack, until it was almost full of water and I was getting a bit panicky. I cried out for help and suddenly there was this great flapping of wings and the sack, along with me inside it was lifted from the water and dumped onto the beach. A sharp beak made a hole large enough for me to get out and there stood my rescuer, a quirky looking bird, who introduced himself as Edwin Razorbill. After lecturing me on the dangers of sailing without a proper boat, he kept a few inquisitive gulls at bay then led me up the beach to where Mr. and Mrs. were having a picnic. They took me home with them and introduced me to Rufus who didn't like the idea of sharing house with me. The disappearing turkey was the last straw, and the rest is history.' Lydia was gobsmacked. 'Yoo arr lucky to be here Rylee, yoo owe yoor life to zis Edween Razorbeel.' I nodded in agreement. 'Yes, he was like a guardian angel, there when I needed him most. But enough about me, Lydia. What's your story? And if I may ask, where has your fur gone?' I hoped she wouldn't be embarrassed or annoyed by my question.

'Zat bit eez zeemple. I am catching rats in zer sheeps bilges and getting covered in diesel oil and seawater every day. Eet makes my fur fall out but it grows back when I am ashore for long time. And before yoo ask about my eyes, I vill tell yoo. My Muzzer voz verking at nuclear vaste factory ven she voz carrying me, and I zink zat iz vot make my eyez not normal. But I can zee better zan most ozzer cats. Zer rest of my life eez not zo zeemple. My muzzer voz Abyssinian, viz beautiful coat and I voz just like her.'

'What about your father?' I asked, 'did you know him?' She shook her head sadly. 'Muzzer zed he voz Chechynian rebel cat leader and had to go fight zumwhere before I voz born.'

'Didn't he return?' I queried.

'No, muzzer zed zat he voz on a mission viz more rebels. Zey were trying to cross a border in Zer Mountains, but zer compass zey had voz broken. Zey vent round and round in circles, until zey finally dizzappeared, never to be zeen again.'

'Where was this?' I asked.

'Zomewhere up zer Khyber Pass, according to my muzzer.'

She fell silent for a moment and a shadow of sadness crossed her face. I don't like silence, so I broke it. 'Is your mother still around?' Her face became even sadder.

'No, she alzo dizzappeared, one night, zomewhere near zer local glove factory, never to be zeen again except maybe on zer hands of zer aristocracy, keeping zem warm.' I was stunned. I had to get her mind off that. 'How did you come to be working on the ships?' 'Vell, a cat haz to eat and most of my relative's verk on feeshing boats. Zumtimes we meet up in different ports and have party. Eet eez not bad life Rylee, and I get to meet a lot of people, like yoo.' I nodded. It was a harder life than mine, that's for sure.

'Do you think that one Day, you might settle down?' She nodded back. 'Yez, one Day I vill, ven it zeems to be zer right time.'

I thought for a minute. 'I hope I will be close by when you do.' She smiled. 'Zat vud be nice, but before yoo get too zerious, vot time eez tea around here? I am feeling razzer peckeesh.' That broke the spell I could feel closing over me. 'Okay, I said, let's go see what Shezza's cooking up.' As we got closer to Shezzas flat, a rather inviting aroma of cooked chicken wafted over us. Belinda and Grace were already there, sat on the parapet at the end of the patio. Shezza was watching out for us. 'There you are, just in time, you two. Belinda and Grace didn't want to start without you, so I'll serve them first.' It was the fastest tour ever, that took all of two minutes, then me and Lydia were queuing up to be served. Shezza piled the food up high while me, Lydia,

Belinda and Grace did our best to put it away. It was hard work but enjoyable.

'Zer chicken voz supreme' said Lydia, 'zank yoo very much.' Belinda and Grace agreed. After we had rested for a while, Shezza brought out bowls of custard with a big blob of fresh cream on top. 'I might burst if I eat all this,' I exclaimed.

'In zat case let us burst togezzer.' Lydia replied. Belinda and Grace did their best to help out.

It was a clear warm evening and the sun was fading slowly. Shezza was relaxing on her lounger, reluctant to go inside while it was so comfortable outside. Belinda and Grace had settled on their chimney stack abode. I looked over at Lydia. She had curled up near Shezzas feet after dinner and remained there still. That's a dangerous place to be sometimes, after she has had a hard day on them, but I suppose Lydia is used to strange odours in the ships bilges. Nevertheless, I gave her a nudge just to check if she was still conscious. 'It's going to be dark soon,' I whispered, 'I'll walk you back to the ship if you like.' Lydia sighed, yawned and stretched. 'Eet eez zo peaceful here, I might stay over and join sheep in zer morning, eef zats okay viz yoo. Repairs may be completed tomorrow, Zen I vill be leaving.' My heart nearly burst through my chest at the thought of her staying over, and almost dropped through my stomach at the thought of her leaving. I had only known this goggle eyed, bald seafaring cat, who wore clothes to cover her missing fur, for a couple of days, but in that short time I had grown to like her.

'Of course it's okay with me, I would like nothing better than the pleasure of your company.'

'Zen vy zer long face Rylee?'

'I was thinking about tomorrow, when you are gone. Things won't be the same without you. Are you sure you won't stay here with us? Shezza won't mind.'

She looked quite serious for a moment.

'To all intentz and pupozez, I am illegal immigrant. Eef harbour master zee me he vill report me to local government officer, and he vill run me out of country.'

'What? Clifton Bladderhead? He wouldn't run a tap without guidance from Westminster, and that could take ages.'

She shook her head. 'Eet vud not be fair to yoo or Shezza but I vill try to keep in touch viz yoo somehow. Now I theenk I need zer ladies room, if yoo vill show me.' Shezza had gone inside now, washing up. We went in and rubbed around her ankles, miaowed our thanks and made our way down to my favourite little park where gardener George had done his best to loosen all the soil around the borders.

'Ladies down that end and gents over here' I proudly announced. George would be pleased when he came in on Monday, to see that all his hard work had not gone unnoticed, and had been well used by us.

'Shall ve valk along zer promenade?' Lydia asked, 'eet eez clear night.' That was okay with me so we strolled along North beach for a while. Behind us, were the bright lights of Brid town centre. Ahead, the promenade lights twinkled in a perfect arc around the bay. Further on, in the shadow of the cliffs, was the Flamborough lighthouse, out on a limb, casting its warning beam across the waves.

Just along the prom, we came upon a couple of cats staring up at the stars. Lydia was wondering who the intelligent looking one was, as he tried to focus the promenade telescope while balancing on the shoulders of his smaller companion.

'Zeez are friendz of yours?'

'Yes, I replied, the one with the telescope, we call him Jupiter, after the planet, because he always has his head in the clouds.'

'And eez leetle friend?'

'That's Uranus, you don't want to know where he has his head.'

'Eet eez not alzo in clouds?'

'Er, no, much lower down than that.' After introducing Lydia to them and trying to convince Jupiter that she wasn't from another solar system, we bade them goodnight. Jupiter tapped the side of his nose as he gazed mesmorised, at the reflection of the stars in Lydia's goggly eyes, and winked. 'Your secret is safe with me,' he whispered. 'May I wish you a safe and speedy journey Home?'

'Zank yoo very much, eet weel take maybe three days.'

'Wow! That is speedy!'

'Az long az zer engine duz not fail again, ve vill make good time. Eet eez only broken engine that make uz stop here, and zen I meet viz Rylee and he show me round zis place.' Jupiter was overwhelmed with all the wrong ideas.

'Remember us when you get back to your own galaxy.'

'Oh I vill, how can I forget meeting yoo, I vill make full report to my flight commander.' While Jupiter was lost for words and overcome with emotion, I dragged her away. 'Don't encourage him, he's been watching out for space visitors for years.'

' Eet eez just my leetle joke.' She replied.

We made our way back to my little park garden and found a comfy place to relax. I was contented. Lydia was contented. Belinda and Grace were contented as they looked down on us from their penthouse cum chimney. We gazed up at the stars and the whole world could be contented, for all I knew. I turned to Lydia and she held out her paws and cuddled me. I cuddled her. Belinda and Grace cuddled. Even the stars seemed to cuddle, as we drifted off into a deep comfortable slumber.

ELEVEN.

JULY 2014. *FAREWELL……A day of reckoning.*

I was enjoying a really good dream where lots of fish were jumping out of the harbour and landing at my feet, when suddenly they all opened their mouths and made a sound like a street sweeping machine. I forced my eyes open and found that the noise was for real. Sweeper Sam drove slowly past the gardens while Roadside Bob emptied the bins with a great clattering. Why do they start so early? For Pete's sake, its only 6am, but Brid cleansing dept. want every speck of litter cleared before a ray of sunlight can touch it. I looked around for Lydia. She was up on a bench, with a paw cupped to her ear. 'I Zeenk I hear sheep's siren calling all hands back! Engine must be mended! I must go Rylee!' I was still half asleep when she planted a smacker on my cheek then set off down the prom like a bat out of hell, leaving only the smell of burning rubber from her little red boots lingering on the fresh sea air. I tried gathering my wits about me but they kept drifting off again, so I just set out after her, dazed, as quickly as I could. There was no way that I could catch up, and as I reached the harbour entrance she was running up the gangplank and climbing aboard the fishing vessel. Thick smoke billowed from the funnel and the water began to churn as the engines started to push it toward the open sea. Lydia suddenly appeared at the stern. As I ran toward her she threw something onto the dockside and waved. 'For yoo Pushkin.' She carried on waving as the ship left the harbour and I thought it must be raining as great wet blobs dripped down my cheeks. Oh, no, it's not rain, it's my eyes leaking. They haven't done that for a long time. Quickly drying them in case any of Jelly's mob were up early and saw me, I made my way to the end of the dock to see what Lydia had thrown. It was a nice portion of Cod. Oh, my, it made my day, but the great lump in my throat made it difficult to swallow.

Climbing the harbour wall at the very end, I watched the ship until it became a speck on the horizon, oblivious to everything around me. Belinda and Grace drifted down from the sky and landed on the wall beside me.
'Don't be fretting now Riley,' Grace whispered, 'She will be back sooner or later,' I hoped it would be sooner. Belinda squawked a warning as she and Grace flapped furiously away. The hairs on the back of my neck began to bristle, and as I turned, every hair on my body followed suit. Standing before me was the biggest, ugliest fearsome looking cat. More like a mountain Lion really, with a patch over one eye, and scars in abundance. He stood tall, arms folded, blocking my exit. Behind him was, guess who? Yes, Jellybone Frazer, who else? He grinned at me as he announced, 'This is my cousin Marcel, you may have heard of him Riley.' *I have heard of him I thought. Mad Marcel, the cutthroat*

from Algiers. What the heck was he doing here? I asked myself. The smirk on Jelly's ugly mush answered for me. 'I sent word to my cousin, that I was having a hard time keeping you in line, Riley. He very kindly offered to teach you some manners. Bye for now,' he laughed, as he backed away, giving Marcel room to flex his muscles. 'Sorry I can't hang around but I just can't stand the sight of blood.'

That left little ole me facing the muscle bound self - employed pain distributor. I looked for a way out and wished I had paid more attention when Belinda and Grace were trying to teach me to fly. The Tide was beginning to turn, and the last of the fishing boats were going out with it. It would be too strong a current for me to swim against around the harbour and on to the beach. I probably wouldn't make it. No running away, I decided. Actually I didn't have a choice. Somebody once said that the best line of defence is to attack. And that's just what I did. While he was going through his routine of cracking his knuckles and loosening up, I launched myself at his head, claws outstretched. He batted me away with one great paw, as I took a swipe at his ugly mug. My claws caught on his eye patch, ripping it from his head. With the eye patch gone he looked worse than ever. The empty eye socket cast a dark shadow across one side of his face highlighting vicious scars from previous battles. His mouth drew back in a snarl exposing his fangs. Each fang had been capped with sharp metal which glinted in the sunlight. As he drew closer he pulled back hard on his paws. I gasped at the exposed two inch long claws as they clicked open and shut, like a hungry lobster approaching its prey. Marcel had obviously paid a visit to Madam Foo Foo's on the High street and was now sporting a set of her finest titanium claw extensions. I admired the pretty colour for a moment, thinking he could have chosen something other than cherry red, or was it blood? It would soon be my blood if I didn't do something quickly. The only thing I felt like doing was emptying my bowel as he finished limbering up. I didn't have time for that. He was almost upon me when I got this stupid notion to stand up to him. Taking a deep breath and clutching my buttocks together, I prepared myself to become mincemeat. Up on my toes and tall as possible, I stared him in the knees.

Marcel paused, looking me over like a butcher deciding where to make the first cut. Belinda and Grace had been circling above us but suddenly took flight toward Flamborough. Great! I thought, maybe they can't stand the sight of blood either. Marcel crouched, like a Sumo wrestler closing in for the kill. Something caught my eye above and beyond him. A trio of birds flying in close formation. Two of them looked like Belinda and Grace. I couldn't make out the third as it began to fly higher than the other two. I cupped my paws over my eyes to try and focus on it. Marcel snarled 'that's the oldest trick in the book Riley, there is no one behind me.'

The unknown bird was flapping its wings furiously as it started to descend, then tucked them to its sides and took on the shape of an arrow as it plummeted from the sky. I'm not sure if I heard a sonic boom, it was travelling so fast. But I did hear the words 'E-D-W-I-N- R-A-Z-O-R-B-I-L-L TO THE RESCU-U-u-u-u' just before he made contact with Marcels backside at somewhere around speed Mach five. The world seemed to stand still for a moment, everything froze for a tenth of a second. Then, in what seemed like slow motion, Marcel sailed clear over my head. I saw the agony on his mush, heard the scream and the crunch as he flipped over the sea wall, catching his head as he went, and then the sickening thud as he landed, not in the water, but on the deck of the last departing trawler heading out into the North Sea. When he wakes up, he will be in splints for weeks, by which time he might be in Outer Mongolia or somewhere similar, I hope.

My rescuer lay in a dishevelled heap, shaking his head feebly, struggling to speak. 'I flink I bloke my bleak,' he whimpered. I knelt down and checked him over.
 'No, you haven't broken your beak. It's just a bit, er, crumpled. That's twice you have rescued me Edwin, you really are my guardian angel, but there really was no need. I had it all under control and was just about to

79

make my move when you stepped in.' *I tried to sound convincing.* 'Thank you for saving me the trouble though, how can I ever repay you?'

He shook his head. 'You looked like you were praying for a miracle to me, but just get me back to Bempton Cliff's sanctuary, I'm getting too old for all this.' Then his body crumpled, just like his beak. Belinda and Grace searched around until they found a cardboard box at the rear of the harbour café, to put him in. We took turns pushing and shoving it until we left the harbour and got to the main road. 'It's a long way to Bempton, can we smuggle him onto a bus? Belinda asked. Just then, the answer to our prayers came screeching along the prom, scattering people in all directions. Ferrari Fred stamped on the brakes when he saw us and looked into the box. 'That bird needs to get to the sanctuary at Bempton,' he exclaimed. 'Let me get him into my basket and I'll have him up there in no time'. Before you could say 'burning rubber' we were all perched on Fred's mobility scooter and breaking land speed records all the way to Bempton. Once Edwin was settled at the sanctuary, Belinda and Grace flew back to town, saying they had business to attend to. I hitched a lift in Fred's basket all the way back to the harbour with the wind parting my hair and flattening my ears. There seemed to be a great gathering of gulls working their way along the prom toward South Beach, diving and swooping at something in their midst. Belinda and Grace appeared from the squawking crowd and flew over when they saw me. 'We got a few friends together, to run Jellybone Frazer out of town for good!' At the rate they were going, he would be in Hull before nightfall. Good riddance to him, I thought. Things can only get better around here now. After such a hectic start to the day, I suddenly felt tired, weak and empty. Running on adrenalin doesn't suit me. I'd rather run on a full stomach. Or better still, not run at all. Getting myself back into lazy cat mode was the order of the day, and so I headed home. I can't believe that Lydia has gone. There's an empty space at my side that needs filling. There's also an empty space inside me that needs filling, with food! Shezza was hanging out washing when I slunk onto the patio. 'Where have you been all night my little love?' she said, while showering me with hugs and kisses. 'And where's your new friend? Has she gone home then? Oh my, your eyes look a bit weepy, I hope you haven't got a chill.' And with that she carried me inside, fed and pampered me, until I fell asleep.

TWELVE

August 2014.   *All's well...*

Four long weeks have passed since Lydia sailed away. Edwin Razorbill is fully recovered and has my undying gratitude. His beak has straightened out, so now he can feed himself without the aid of the nice people at the rescue centre. There have been no reported sightings of Jellybone Frazer or his scurvy mates. Neither have there been any of Lydia, nor the trawler that she works on. All the cats on the waste bin circuit moved up a step. Limpalong Lennie is now in charge of the gutting shed bins and makes sure that any hungry cats get fed. I spend some of my spare time down there, putting the world to rights with him, while keeping an eye on the ships coming in, just in case you know who turns up.

On market days I walk Shezza to work and wait for her on the nearest stall to the café. That's the stall of Bogroll Benny, with a sign that says he brings 'cheap and tender comfort to the delicate cheeks of the North East.' He also shares his dinner with me and in return, if things are a bit quiet, I jump up on his stall and start juggling the toilet rolls. That usually brings in the crowds and while they are enthralled with me, Benny gives them the spiel and money changes hands. Sometimes, just to pass the time and keep the punters happy, Benny strums his guitar. I join in and sing them a song I made up about Lydia.

'Have you seen Lydia, she's from Abyssinia,

L-y-d-i-a my g-ogg-l-e-y-e-d girlfriend

She purrs down the street, red boots on her feet

L-y-d-i-a my g-o-gg-le-y-e-d girlfriend

People all stare, cos she's got no hair,

L-y-d-i-a my g-o-gg-l-e-y-e-d girfriend

And they wonder why, she's got two glass eyes

That's L-y-d-i-a - my- g-o-gg-l-e-y-e-d girlfriend!

Lydiarnavich Gregorina Lubyanska.

'The finest ratter working the North Seas.'

When I start singing, the crowd put their fingers in their ears. Benny says it's to show that they are listening, as they are not allowed to clap in public places due to a new ruling from the noise abatement society. Then he gets a couple of sausages from his lunchbox for me to chew on while he struggles on, trying to entertain them alone. It all brings the working day to an end. Then Shezza appears with a cake for Benny and a cuddle for me.

We leave Benny packing up his stall and head for home. Sometimes we walk along the beach so that Shezza can get some fresh air to her feet after being on them all day. Her shoes heave a sigh of relief as she kicks them off and her feet swell to twice their normal size. She paddles along the edge of the surf, contaminating the local habitat and raising the sea temperature a few degrees. The chances of us getting a blue flag award on the beach, depends entirely on the state of Shezza's feet. If our MP. Clifton Bladderhead knew, he would probably put a restraining order on her, confining her to the promenade.

I trail along behind her, letting the gentle waves swirl around my paws while helping any stunned crabs get back under their rocks. It's always a pleasant way to end the day. The weather is wonderful and the beaches are very popular right now. It's the middle of school holidays and I think half the families in Yorkshire are here despite my trying to keep this place a secret. Maybe I'll do a bit of surfing tomorrow, or sunbathe and check out the inside of my eyelids. Some days I just sit on the prom and watch all the people enjoying themselves in various ways. It can be really fascinating.

Home at last. Belinda and Grace greet us as usual and we all look forward to tea. Then Shezza can put her feet up for a while before setting out to her second job. I might try and get a paper round to help her out. Then she could relax for a while and find more time to enjoy herself.

I really must get round to the job centre and see what they have on offer for an intelligent smart looking cat like me. Mattress testing would be my first choice, followed closely by chicken tasting on behalf of the local supermarket, just to make sure that the quality is up to standard. All this thought about work has made me quite sleepy. I'll think about it properly tomorrow when I'm down on the beach helping visitors to finish their sandwiches off.

As I drift off to sleep I can't help thinking what a strange year this has been so far, and it's only August. Just a few months and it will be turkey time again.

Bye for now.

        Riley Anthony.

Printed in Great Britain
by Amazon

85311993R00051